I know a secret

illustrated by Annie Kubler

Child's Play (International) Ltd

© M. Twinn 1988   ISBN 0-85953-315-8   Printed in Singapore

I know
where babies
come from!

Huh! Boys
don't know
anything!

They come from Mummy's tummy.

My Mum's got a baby
in her tummy now.

Don't be silly!
How can a baby
be in there?

I was a big baby.

There is room.
Part of Mummy's tummy
is called a uterus.
The baby grows in there
in a sac filled with liquid.
As the baby grows,
the tummy stretches.

Liquid?
A baby isn't a fish.

Anyway, what do Daddies do?

My Mum said,
when she and Daddy wanted me,
they made a sand pie
and put a mustard seed in it.

That's not how you make a baby.

You need Mummy's egg
and a seed from Daddy.
When they come together,
that's when the baby starts.

It's smaller than
a grain of sand.

Look! I've got a baby
on my finger!

I've just thought of
something else.
How do babies grow?

What do babies eat?
Where do they get food from?
Do they drink the liquid?

And how do they breathe?

I don't know. I'll ask my Mum.

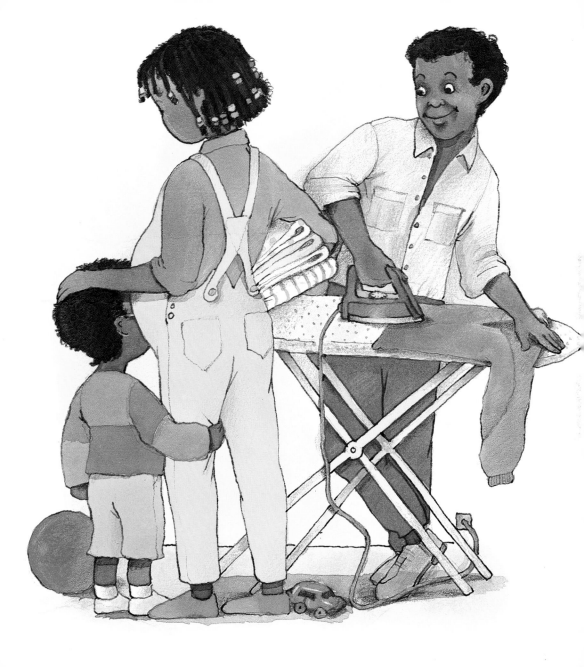

Hey, kids! I've got the answer!
I know how babies feed and breathe!
Come on, my Dad is going to
take us for a ride.

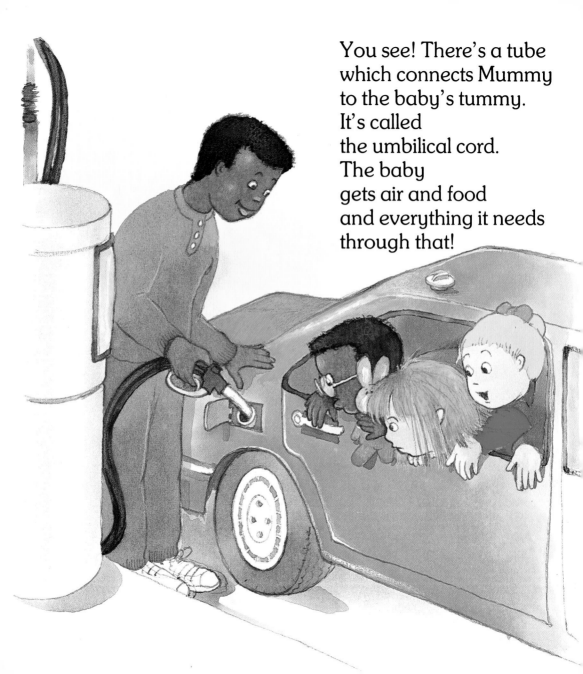

You see! There's a tube which connects Mummy to the baby's tummy. It's called the umbilical cord. The baby gets air and food and everything it needs through that!

It must be boring being a baby!
What does it do all day?
It doesn't play. It can't see.
Does it just float about?

My Mummy says
it's nice being a baby.
It's warm and comfortable
in the uterus and
the baby can feel that
it is loved.

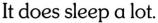
It does sleep a lot.

It does move
its little arms
and legs about.

It sucks its thumb.

It likes to listen
to Mummy's voice
and to music.

The bigger it gets,
the more it kicks
to let you know it's there.

If it's so good in there,
why does the baby
want to come out?

It grows too big.

Tell me, clever clogs,
if it is as big as that,
how does it get out?

When the baby is ready,
it pushes its way out.
Head first!

Our baby will
be doing that soon.

Mummy has a passage between her legs.
It stretches just like your knickers do.
See!

When it is out,
the doctor cuts
the umbilical cord.

That's why we've got
a belly button.
That's where the cord was.

Sorry, I can't play.
I've got to look after baby.

She's lovely!

I want a baby!